Chris Redmond is a spoken wor(dabbler. A regular at UK music an(featured on BBC Radio 1, BBC F Arts. Sometimes he goes deep (i to splash around happily in the sh but skinnier and without the prongy bit.

Chris is the creator and frontman of Tongue Fu, one of the UK's leading spoken word shows, where poets, comedians, storytellers and rappers perform with improvised music and films.

> 'Poetry, but not as you know it ... amazing.'
> The Guardian

As a musician Chris has toured extensively with all kinds of reprobates. In the slightly more respectable world of theatre he has worked with Improbable on *Panic*, ice&fire on *The Nine O'Clock Slot* and with Cecilia Knapp on her show *Finding Home*, and has composed music for EMI/KPM, BBC One, ITV and Discovery Channel.

As an educator, Chris leads workshops in writing, performing and musicianship for organisations such as the British Council, BBC, BAC, National Theatre, the Roundhouse and St Mary's University, Twickenham, where he leads a module called Political Cabaret on the Applied Theatre degree.

www.chrisredmond.co.uk

www.tonguefu.co.uk

Let the Pig Out

Chris Redmond

Burning Eye

Copyright © 2016 Chris Redmond

The author asserts the moral right under the Copyright, Designs and Patents Act 1988 to be identified as the author of this work.

All rights reserved. No part of this publication may be reproduced, stored in a retrieval system, or transmitted, in any form or by any means without the prior written consent of the author, nor be otherwise circulated in any form of binding or cover other than that in which it is published and without a similar condition being imposed on the subsequent purchaser.

This edition published by Burning Eye Books 2016

www.burningeye.co.uk
@burningeyebooks

Burning Eye Books
15 West Hill, Portishead, BS20 6LG

ISBN 978 1 90913 6 694

Let the Pig Out

CONTENTS

DARTMOOR	10
SPEED FREAK	11
FORD TRANSCENDENTAL	14
A COCK ON THE FROME ROAD	17
BIRD PENIS	18
PETER AND THE FOX	19
WAITING	22
WAVES (A LETTER TO LULA, MARCH 2011)	23
LET THE PIG OUT	26
GEOGRAPHY LESSON	29
BROGUE BOP	31
RUSS IN A DREAM	32
DEAD FRIEND(S)	33
LIMINAL	34
HIDE	36
EXISTENTIAL DOCTOR	37
SEEING A NOSEBLEED AS AN OPPORTUNITY FOR CATHARSIS	40
IN THE KEY OF G	42
PORTRAIT OF THE ARTIST AS A NEW DAD	46
SUPPERTIME	50
GRAMMAR WARS WITH A TWO-YEAR-OLD	51
PRAYER IN THE VALLEY	54
PATRICIA	55
LIKE DRAGONS (BIRTHDAY LETTER TO SELF)	56
FIRES	58

Dedicated to Peter and Pat.

DARTMOOR

When you remove the lid
from a jar that has rested, inert,
for blank time on some dusty shelf,
you can almost hear the gulping
as it sucks in fresh air.

It was the same driving here,
watching the grey light,
the moors,
the oaks and bracken, heavy with rain.

I wound down the window,
cold air on my tired face,
opened my mouth,
inhaled.

Drove through a deep puddle.
Splashed cold mud inside my mouth.
Cursed my attempt at spirituality.

SPEED FREAK

Quick fixes.

Speed dating, instant messaging,
SlimFast, fast lane,
nought to sixty in three seconds
in a thirty-mile-an-hour zone.
Speed dial, sat nav,
voice recognition on my phone.
Twitter tweets twats' facts.
Endless data stream
of collective unconscious.
Wade through
up-to-the-minute news feeds,
sports results beamed
direct to the brain,
one thousand and twenty-six apps
telling me where and when
is my next train.
I can
simultaneously
watch three films, nine TV programmes,
publish my blog, update my website,
Skype chat, Snapchat, WhatsApp,
send mails from all forty-three of my accounts,
link all my posts on
facespacemyplaceyourfacemyarse,
mow the grass, learn kung fu Neo-style,
flash fry a steak, meditate,
write a poem, make love,
do the recycling.

Sod that.

I'm done with it.
Please bring me back to what I know.
If this is the future, good luck, you run with it,
but I am reclaiming slow.
The revolution starts here.

In a bit.

Slow
        is the new fast.
Slow
        is the new cool.

First thing I'm going to do
is set up a new messaging service.
I'm going to get me a mule.
A really lazy one
who's not in a hurry,
who clip-clops along,
me on the back, wearing flip-flops,
singing a song.
I figure the slower you go,
the less need to worry.

It's going to be hip to be slow.
Speed is so done.
I'm going to have It girls calling me up, saying,

'Hi, yah, I hear you're the one?
I need to get a message to someone,
less *allegro*, more *largo*.
I don't want them thinking I'm in a rush,
that's so over.
How slow can you go?'

I'll tell them, 'I'll go as slow as you need.'

'Oh, wow! How do you do it?'

Next, I'm going to stop time.
I'm building a transmitter
that will jam all watches and clocks.
We'll look to the sun again,
think in seasons and crops.

We'll arrange to meet, not at the drop of a tweet
or a text or even at quarter past ten,
but when the sun is at its highest,
four days after full moon.

Then I suggest, when someone asks,
'When will you be here?'/'When will it be done?'
we just answer,
'Soon.'

Half past five, quarter to nine and other familiar times
will be consigned to museums.
They will each be kept in their own shiny glass case.
We will stare at them and see them for the abstracts they are.

Cars will be designed with a second and third gear
in reverse. Each one progressively slower,
so you go so slow backwards,
you eventually start to go forwards again
but with a whole new dimension in between to consider.

The gap between now and then
will get bigger and bigger
until finally, only now
will exist once more.
And the people will wonder
what all the rushing has been for.

If we remove time
then all that's left is

     space.

As Sun Ra said,

     space

is the place.

There's only one pace left to go.
This greed for speed is exceeding its need.
Whoever reaches the future first
might just find it
slow.

FORD TRANSCENDENTAL

People who believe in God can see miracles everywhere. I don't believe in God, or miracles, but I saw one. On the M3, just outside Farnborough.

It is everything a February morning in England promises to be. Sky the kind of grey that scowls at you, rain in sheets, wipers flip-flopping.

I'm driving my red Nissan Micra. Traffic is thick. I'm in the outside lane. The radio is broken, so I am nodding my head to the flick of the wipers mixed with the regular thump of air compressed between the car and the central reservation.

You know those drivers who let you know they want to pass by arriving at your rear bumper as if they are Batman and *YOU NEED TO MOVE OR BE ELIMINATED!?* This Ford Transit, headlights glaring, is one of those. I touch my brakes. He backs off, then lurches forward again. I curse him and pull into the middle lane. Transit sucks up the road.

Two men lean forward, staring at me, expressing through sign language their firm belief that I am a keen masturbator. I raise my index and middle fingers to my nostrils, inhale, then point the fingers at them, as if to say,

I can smell you.

They look confused. I wink. They drive on.

The sun cuts through the grey and, like a smiling god of hippies and children's TV shows, a perfect rainbow shimmies into view, all jazz hands and hope, as if it has no idea of the dull environment it is illuminating.

I've never seen the end of a rainbow. I thought they didn't exist, but this is tantalisingly close, right at the edge of the motorway, hidden only by a cluster of trees and a small car dealership. And as the road turns south-easterly, the end of the rainbow, the actual end of the rainbow hits the opposite carriageway and I'm thinking,

Could it? Could we?

The road twists again. Colours bounce off the central reservation like camp sparks in the rain. Everyone on the M3 slows, even the Transit wankers in front. Then they're in it. Their filthy silver van is shrouded in rainbow spray.

I imagine the conversation.

Bri: Fuck me, Tel. We're in a fuckin' rainbow.
Tel: Yeah.
Bri: I have no superlatives to describe the fuckin' wonder I am currently experiencing.
Tel: Yeah.
Bri: Look, Tel. Look at the world around us, the grey of the road, how the rain hits the windscreen like bullets and the uniformity of the white lines, on and on and on… and yet, this, now, us, Tel. Fuckin' *us*? In a fucking rainbow!
Tel: Yeah.
Bri: I've got tears, Tel. When I tell my daughter I've drove through the end of a rainbow she'll look at me like I'm some sort of magician. This is what the ancients wondered at. Imagine seeing this with no idea why. What sort of god would conjure a vision so ethereal, so full of colour when all the world is rain and grey? Look around us, Tel. These fleeting moments are dragonflies in our hearts. They are the songs the earth sings to us. Where the fuck are we?
Tel: Just coming up to the Bracknell turn-off, Bri.

Then they're through it and it's my turn. For a few seconds all my cynicism drops like heavy clothes.

The air is colour. Wipers smear prism after prism. My eyes feel older, like every shade of the light's pigment is a tone in a lost language I may have once known.

Then it's over. Grey returns. The Transit wankers in front move left to the middle lane. I pull up level with them.

The driver and I look at each other. I point upwards as if to say,

Did you see that?

He narrows his eyes, smiles. Raises his index and middle fingers to his nose, inhales and points them back at me.

A COCK ON THE FROME ROAD

A pheasant ran under my car and died.
I felt sorrow.
I took it home,
wondered sadly at its bright feathers
and prehistoric feet.
Thought about its voice in the fields,
what it had seen with its black eyes.
Turned it over in my hands,
felt its weight.
I could smell its wild life: muddy,
feral,
free.

Skinned it,
rubbed it with butter,
popped it in the oven.

BIRD PENIS

If my penis was a stork or a heron,
such would be its strength and span
that when it flew,
I would be dragged
through treetops
and moist air,
an ungainly cargo
dangling from my root.

Pink skin
would stretch taut,
up pencil-thin legs
and knobbly knees,
to belly, breast
and wings
that callopped,
shlucking the air,
hoisting and lifting.

I would forever drag.
It would forever lead me
across rivers and marshes,
bridges and grasses.
A thin veined featherless Gollum.
Fleshy beak
and eyes for fishy catch.
A small trout here,
a tench, a bream.

Solemn keeper
of a tall, elegant, bird-shaped member,
with a wingspan of four feet or more
and a ten-inch beak,
forever jabbing,
foraging, for frogs
and minnows.

PETER AND THE FOX

Pete devours North London's streets at 2am.
Rubber razor wheels,
aluminium feathers.
Head down, piston legs, he flies.

Pete is twenty.
Tatty trilby, whiskers,
searching bright eyes.
Mind of a scientist,
body of an athlete,
spirit of a Tottenham shaman.
Head down, piston legs, he flies.

October's iron mist
strikes his hungry lungs
as the road rises and twists under him.
He turns a bend,
sees a fox.
Fingers reach for brakes,
foot drops to floor.
He pulls up quietly
and watches.

The fox is twenty feet away,
sniffing some bins.
It catches Pete's scent,
turns towards him.
They both stare,
still,
measuring.

Lustrous rust red, whiskers twitching,
Foxy cocks its slender head, curious,
then saunters in Pete's direction.

Stops.

Sniffs the air.
Trots.

Stops again,
ten feet away.
Six feet,
five,
four,
three,
then the fox is at his feet,
sniffing his socks.

'Oi!'
Pete jumps back.

Foxy looks amused.

Unsure now what to do,
Pete pedals off slowly.
The fox follows.

Pete smiles and pushes up a gear.
The fox follows, throws him a glance
that seems to say,

What have you got, bicycle boy?

Peter digs a little deeper.
The fox's amble switches to a run at his side,
mouth wide, tongue to the night air.

'Alright,' Pete mutters.
'There's a park, half a mile ahead. Race you.'

Cogs mesh with oiled chain.
Fox's body lowers.
Gears switch cleanly, foot and thigh.
Ears back, tail straight behind.
Blood surges.
Heads down, piston legs, they fly.

They fly like the night has suddenly come alive.

Heroes cheered by empty streets
for crossing a divide. They fly.

Pedals, tyres, nails and paws hit a rhythm.
Pete tries to edge forward
but the fox matches everything it's given.

Lungs are white heat, and Pete's screaming, 'COME ON!'
Teeth, fur, feet, blur, locked, neck and neck, push. 'COME ON!'

They fireball past parked cars, fences, signs,
a bus stop and tired houses.
The burn arouses streaming wild eyes.
The burn arouses screaming wild cries.
Pete shouts, fox barks, dead heat.
The park looms left suddenly, end of street,
and the fox darts towards it.

Pete's brakes burn,
he skids, turns, stops,
gulping in air.
Looks back at fox.
It meets his stare.
For a heartbeat
neither knows himself from the other.

Pete shivers,
laughs
like a firework.

The fox turns
and pads into the bushes.

WAITING

These days are honey. Waiting
has never tasted this sweet.

Each morning is a quiet footstep
on the path to our meeting.

We've seen you
through the sonographer's eye,
tiny heart pulsing,
neurons being born like stars
in a nebula. Spine,
a ladder to the past.

At night, before sleep
we gaze at the paunch
where you incubate
and wait, like children at a magic show,
for your wriggles, thrusts,
elbows, head and knees
rippling around taut skin
like that scene in *Alien*.
Your weirdness bewitches.

With breath held,
we know something of alchemy.
We are puppets
and whatever pulls our strings
is so old,
we don't know ourselves.

Each day is the last of that,
the first of this.

Pivot.
Pendulum.
Poise.

WAVES (A LETTER TO LULA, MARCH 2011)

Show me your hands.
I want to see my future.
This is no clairvoyance;
you smell of life after me.
Your eyes intone prayers.
Iris paths to distant laughs, songs,
love and storms. Time
is soft rain. Listen,
we can hear it falling.

What have you brought here?
I am awash. Love,
like a warm serum. This
is water from spring's first melt on my tongue,
the sun's rays in every drop for eternity.
When you open your tiny lips
and our noses touch,
I inhale you,
right to my ancient core.
I am born with you.
Living, all over again.

Time is soft rain,
but its clocks are manifold.
Second hand, minute hand,
hourglass sands slip.
While you snuffle at 3am feed,
our whole planet holds its breath,
as Fukushima Daiichi
lumbers and groans.
A wounded dragon,
venting steam that sours the cold air,
in a nation wailing from Earth's whip crack,
scattering steel, brick and bone
like matchsticks.

Roiling black sea,
devouring towns and cities
like a furious curse.

I turn my face from the screen.
You suckle, plump cheeks pressed
to plump breast.
You sniffle and cry
while thousands stare. Wide
wet eyes. Pray,
mutter, shake their heads.

There is a song that says
all we need is love. I want so much
to tell you it's true.
But right now, my gentle fish,
a broad-faced general with a vengeful heart
is machine-gunning his own people,
screaming them into subservience.
He spits fury like he has fire for teeth,
riddled by power like a cancer,
pockmarked by the poison he spits.

And our leaders sit, drinking
each other's vitriol like easy milk,
blood on their soft hands,
billions richer
from the weapons they sold him.
They castigate
and moralise,
tear open Africa's warm skies,
pour fire on fire
like fickle gods.

Float west on the breeze from this bloodletting.
Two thousand miles to the sea.
Another power roars. A man
clings so meanly to it,
his soldiers are shooting women
by the score,
in his name.

This is pattern.
This is what we have woven.
You are born into a time of waves.
Anthropocene seas are rising,
footsteps are heavy.
The air is loaded
with the weight of promises
left to rot,
to rust.

And this is not the gift
I want to give you.
It's not what I want you to learn about.
But the ground is shifting
and you will only know it as it is.

I search your eyes for where you've come from.
Every ancestor I never knew. The breath
that precedes the telling of every story.

This rain is ours.
Hold my hand.

LET THE PIG OUT

Eddie is twelve years old and timid.
I'm teaching him the drums
but there's something lacking.

I say, Eddie,
your hi-hats are steady,
snare's rocking the two and four,
bass drum's pushing off beats.
It's red raw,
but you've got meat on the bone now.
But Eddie, tell me what you're drumming for,
because these beats are not fat-back.
They're not even a wet slap.
You can't cook at this temperature.

It's said a drummer can summon spirits
from Africa's pulsing core, whose voices
have been echoing through every generation
since our ancestors first stood on two feet.
But right now you're pushing this beat around
like food on a plate you haven't had to work for.
Like a too-polite, under the breath, apologetic,
ever so, *thank you, please, could I?*
Should I? Play it… like… this?

Eddie, whoever's holding you down,
I'm taking their foot off your neck,
so look up.
Untether yourself.
We need to make libations to the drum gods.
Drink, I'll summon them.
We need to light a fire here,
wrap ourselves in smoke. Remember,
this is wood in your hands
and the polymer you strike
still holds the moniker of skin.
Not long ago, calves died
for you to play beats on their hide,

so at least do them the honour
of playing with a passion
befitting of such a sacrifice.

Eddie. Let the pig out.

Eddie says, 'What do you mean?'

Let the pig out.
There's no other way to say it.
Let the pig out.
It's all about how you play
this grunty, funky,
heavy-arsed, munchy,
angry stink of a
muddy-guts, pink or
white or black with a
hairy fat belly. Let the
pig out, Eddie, let the
beats get smelly.
Let the pig out.

Let the hi-hats splash,
get the snare drum cracking.
Push the beat across the bar,
then kick the fucker back in.
Let the pig out.

That pig is Gullinbursti,
steed of Norse god Freyr,
who spreads light through the land
with his golden hair.
That pig pulls Marici,
Buddhist goddess of the heavens,
all-seeing, holding the sun
and moon in her hands.
That pig belongs to Set,
brother and enemy of Osiris.
Set becomes the god

of chaos and darkness.
That pig is Varaha,
incarnation of Vishnu,
who fought and won a thousand-year
battle to save the Earth, Eddie,
and it's you, c'mon,
the pig is inside.
And when you release the beast,
cast your worries to one side.
It'll untie your tongue-tie,
trample your burden.
The pig is your friend, Eddie.
Of that much I'm certain.
Let the pig out.

To the kid getting bullied at school
'cause he's different. Let the pig out.

To the girl with a song in her heart
but no one to sing to. Let the pig out.

To every artist, writer, dancer,
poet, musician. Let the pig out.

To the people around the world
standing up for change. Let the pig out.

To the nurse who lost her job
so the banker can keep his bonus. Let the pig out.

To the widow who learns beyond grief,
there's a choice. Let the pig out.

To the bipolar explorer choosing
adventure and medication. Let the pig out.

To every little Eddie,
finding a voice.

GEOGRAPHY LESSON

Mr George,
I never knew your first name
but I will always remember your moustache.
A wire wool aberration,
a tangled brush of grey piano wires,
besmirching the good work and style
of Burt Reynolds and David Soul
the decade before.
You dragged
the 'tache into the late eighties, doggedly,
like the reluctant school children
upon whom you so gleefully inflicted
your enthusiasm for geography.

I'm forty-two.
You must be pushing seventy.
I can still smell
the stale Nescafé
on your breath.
Whenever I hear a Belfast accent, the words
Redmond, out now!
ricochet through my conscience.

I'm on a train.
It's January.
The rains are relentless.
Through the mud-flecked window
I see the swollen Avon
slopping and churning,
its banks submerged,
fields flooded.

I scan the scene for your teachings.
Precipitation – check.
Sedimentation – check.
I can hear your mouth
closing around the vowels,
compacting them
as if crushing coal into diamond.

And there, shimmering in the sodden grass,
the elusive jewel in the GCSE crown
of riverside geographic terminology.

Oxbow lake.

BROGUE BOP

You're a smart pair of fishes.
Box-fresh.
Tissue rustle symphony.
Lid lift, first inhalation,
all oak and dye.
Tan beaten, polished. Eyes
on the past, echoes
of grazing meadows and 1950s
hepcat New York sidewalk shuffle.
Murder, finger click.
Style, finger click.
Jive, finger click.
Jazz, cigarettes,
pork-pie hats
and skin.
Casing of flesh.
Organ of breathing mother,
suckling calf.

If I put my ear to you,
I can hear the wails
of Coltrane
and the slaughterhouse.

RUSS IN A DREAM

In sleep's ether
he wanders in.
Broad shoulders,
red hair,
frown like a question.

Grief dissolves,
sluices like a flash flood
from my heaving chest.
Joy weakens me,
stuns my blinking eyes.

We hug,
brothers again
for those few moments.
I inhale
and hold him
and hold him.

DEAD FRIEND(S)

Empty
of taste. Tongue,
just meat now.

Empty
of want. Desire,
a flat line.

Empty
of blood. Skin,
a cold cloth.

A cracked cup
no longer holding
water or tea.

A cracked record,
arrested funk,
beatless.

A broken promise
of laughter.

LIMINAL

Out here, it's dawn and dusk.
Shadows are thin.
The universe bears down.
Words are diaphanous.

Out here, every smile sings the body
electric, like Whitman said.
Every look charged with knowing
this all ends.

Let's take off our coats,
feel the weak sun on our backs.
Let's eat fried egg sandwiches by the river at 7am
and share the crusts with the ducks and fishes.

Out here, there are cracks in the lens.
Every artifice seems rigid, silly.
The day's headlines are flotsam, watch them drift.
The water flows quickly.

Tell me what your life is,
what you're making of it,
because this light
gives its colour to love.

Tell me what your life is,
how you are playing.
Is there any way you can split through your own skin
and sit here, raw nerves in the frigid air?

Is there?

Breathing

Blinking

Listening

You know,
ice is melting two thousand miles away,
an elk breathes mist into snowy morning,
a doctor queues for bread between bomb craters,
croissants are fresh at Liverpool Street station,
a key turns, petrol becomes flame,
soldiers rape a girl while her sister watches,
crows pick flesh from the carcass of a fox,
a woman sells fried egg sandwiches for £1.50.

It's dawn.
It's dusk.

HIDE

What are you staring at?
Glass eyes, broken teeth,
nose, split and cracked,
hanging from your face.

I can almost smell the cold air
in the Polish forest that morning.
I can see the drool on your brown jowls,
hear your jaw slupping,
tongue loose, paws padding
as you ambled.

Today, in this shack in Devon,
wood smoke and tea, I'm uneasy
resting my feet on you.
I wonder,
what was the last thing you saw
before the bullet,
before hot pain
and fading.

EXISTENTIAL DOCTOR

Me: Hello, doctor.
Doctor: Hello, Mr Redmond. Come in, take a seat. What can I do for you?
Me: Well, it's my sense of purpose.
Doc: Yes?
Me: It feels a bit slippery, a bit hard to pin down.
Doc: I see. When was the last time you felt it?
Me: Hmm, well, it comes and goes… maybe last Wednesday, but it didn't stay long.
Doc: Was it big or small?
Me: Fairly small.
Doc: Ah, so how far into the future did it stretch?
Me: Hmm… about half an hour…
Doc: Well, that doesn't really sound like a sense of purpose to me, more a niggling feeling of restlessness.
Me: You mean I haven't got a sense of purpose at all?
Doc: I couldn't say for sure, but half an hour is quite short.
Me: How long should it be?
Doc: Usually years, sometimes a lifetime.
Me: Right. Shit. So I have lost it?
Doc: Possibly.
Me: But where?
Doc: Probably the void.
Me: The void? Time eternal? The meaninglessness of all existence when faced with the infinite emptiness of space?
Doc: That's the puppy. It's hard to maintain a sense of purpose sometimes with any sort of awareness of all that. Do you have a God?
Me: No, not for some time.
Doc: When was the last time you had faith?
Me: Ooh, eight or nine years ago.
Doc: And that was faith in an omnipotent being?
Me: Oh, no, just a bit of a dabble in reiki, sound healing and the law of attraction.

Doc: Right. Alternative beliefs, then? Did you see any practitioners or did you get these beliefs from the internet?

Me: I did go on a couple of courses. A few books, some internet research.

Doc: Tsk... if I had a pound for every...

Awkward silence.

Me: So, what do you suggest?

Doc: There are certain exercises you can do to develop a sense of purpose. Or, if you feel like you can live without, there's an almost endless supply of TV and porn online. I often find lifestyle choices are enough to sufficiently dull the desire for a long-term sense of purpose altogether.

Me: But I want one.

Doc: Right, in that case I prescribe a course of action that involves the following three things: writing, talking and doing.

Me: Go on.

Doc: One: write daily to connect with who you are, what you are thinking about and what your story is. A sense of purpose without a belief system is harder to pin down. They can often be found in stories, so write your own. Start with little things and the bigger ideas will come.
Two: talk and listen to people. Share ideas and information. From this you'll be inspired and may feel less alone. Religion provides community with shared goals. Without it, you have to find your people by yourself.
Three: do stuff. See the world, help people, build things, go to the theatre, art galleries, walk the streets, fall in love, have children, teach, dance, play music, learn applied maths, learn a language, swim. You choose.

Me: It's a bit hands-on, isn't it? Isn't there something you could just give me, other than advice? Something to just take the edge off?

Doc: Have you ever watched *Top Gear*?

SEEING A NOSEBLEED AS AN OPPORTUNITY FOR CATHARSIS

Keep it going.
Let the blood run.
Taste the salt on your lips.
Let it drip and hang
from your chin, spit
a little. Observe
the warm flower unfurl
on your white shirt. Relax
as it spreads its petals
like danger.

Cultivate a frown,
a stunned look,
a stagger.
Then sway and bump,
knocking into shoulders.
Groan, mumble apologies, fall

into a fruit and veg stand.
Feel the soft bananas
mould to your elbows; laugh.
Laugh louder,
groan again, roll.
Feel avocado after avocado
yield, launching their stones
like insults,
stinging the shins of passers-by
and if anyone tries to lift you up,
resist.
Shrug them off, thrash.
Shout, 'FUCKING BRIAN!
YOU BASTARD!'
Twice.

Stand.
Straighten yourself.
Shake the fruit

and blood from your hair
like a lion,
like a victory,
like a warning.
And run.

IN THE KEY OF G

John Coltrane knew nothing.
Some say his blistering, plaintive
tenor love songs to the infinite
were hewn from the cosmos itself.
Some say he was sowing fire seeds
for universal consciousness to flower.
Some say his fingers were so fast,
he could generate enough energy
to power half of Manhattan,
just in the opening refrain to 'Giant Steps'.
But let's not get carried away.
Trane didn't have that much to say.

Miles Davis?
Knew even less.
Charlie Parker?
Minnow.
Ellington, Armstrong,
Dizzy, Mingus, Roach, Monk,
Ella, Nina, Lady Day, Sarah Vaughan.
All just steps on the well-worn path
to enlightenment,
to a beautiful sense
of entitlement.

If they could hear the fruits of their labour
embodied in one man, alive today,
they'd smile,
hold their hearts with humble pride
and nod. They'd stare in wonder
at jazz's seventy-five-million-album-selling god.
The man to harness the power of every musician
who burned so bright,
who gave their lives to music,
to lift spirits, to elevate.
Those who, night after night,
would howl their cauldron souls raw
through drums, piano, singing

or blowing a battered dented horn,
pushing each done day hard,
right through to a new dawn.

If truly they could see him,
he who has taken their hard-fought victories
and made them his own, they would ask
in reverence and hushed tones,

'Who is he?'

And I would say, 'He is our saviour.
He is the one with jazz's true flavour.
His name is Kenny G.'

That's the jazz for me.

None of the raging genius
and muscular power of Mingus,
writing his torrid heart into big band hurricanes
and bedding twenty hookers in a night. No.

I want my jazz with a ponytail
and trousers that are too tight.

I want reverb on my sax.
Drums as thin as David Cameron's promises.
Bass like a wet worm.
Keys that wouldn't sound out of turn
on an advert for Daz Automatic.
I want jazz that buzzes with thin, reedy irritation,
like static.
I want it so sickly my teeth fall out.
I want so much erectile dysfunction in my jazz
there's no chance of any actual jazz coming out.

I want my jazz *Starbucks*.
I want it *Richard and Judy*.

I want it so soulless,
even if it rolled over and died
it wouldn't move me.

Water it down, go on.
Stir in some sugar.
Add an extra measure of emptiness.
Here, have my heart,
I don't need it any more.
Kenny tells me what I'm living for.

I don't want acid jazz.
I want flaccid jazz.
I want wilting, smooth, vapid jazz.
I'm done with feeling.
All that pain?
Ewww.
I want my jazz mewled to me
by the bastard offspring
of Michael Bolton and Celine Dion.
The sound of every new-age meditation backing track,
of every wrist-slittingly bland department store.
I want my jazz to wipe the floor
with my hopes. Kenny,
play to me.
Sing me your flaccidity.

As humans grasp
at the last wisps of fertility,
the final waves of progeny,
before the bucket gets too full and we all kick it

(Can we kick it?
Yes, we can),

Kenny, play to me.
You are the soundtrack to our decline,
the death knell tolling, truly

the end is nigh.
Your blandness is an ocean.
Even the fires of hell would spit and fizzle
and Satan would whimper under the girth
of your mediocrity.
Darwin was wrong.
It's survival of the shittest.

The forests are shrinking.
The skies are growing quiet.
Play us out, Kenny.
It's time.

PORTRAIT OF THE ARTIST AS A NEW DAD

The opening shot is a darkened bedroom.
We see me asleep, arms around my wife
and sleeping daughter, Poppy.
I'm dreaming of myself as the artist I once was:
free, wild(ish).
Poppy presses her soft face into mine
and says sleepily, 'I love you, Daddy.'
I stir, smile, snuggle into her.

Then my eyes snap open.

Her words are Warm Comfort,
enemy of my freedom, my autonomy.
Poppy farts and says, 'Aaaaahhh.'
My wife says, 'Morning, love, you making the tea?'

I make tea for the enemy.

Cut to me in the kitchen.
I'm eating Marmite on toast,
reading a book about Tom Waits.
Close-up of my hand, scribbling the words,
Whiskey, Ford Mustang, nipple tassels.
My frown deepens.

Poppy hugs my leg and says,
'Daddy writing. Daddy write with Poppy?'
Shot of us on the kitchen floor
drawing colourful scribbles with crayons, on big paper.
Poppy says, 'Pretty shapes, Daddy.'
I say, 'They're ironic, Poppy.'
She looks at me and sings,
'I've been to Button Moon.'

I free associate.
Moon, space, David Bowie.
The opening riff of a new song
sneaks into my head.
I shut my eyes, start humming to myself.

Hmmm da da da, da daa

'DADDY!'

Hmmm da da da, da daa

'DADDY!'

Hmmm da da da, da daa

'DAAAAADDDDDYYYY!'

I open my eyes.
I'm staring at Poppy's bum, winking at me.
She's just pissed on my hand.

Cut to another morning. I'm up early,
rifling through the presets
on my distortion pedal.
Lyrics about friendly mice
keep trying to sneak into my brain:

Friendly Mouse, Friendly Mouse,
you are my best friend in the world.

I push them away,
revelling in the feedback.
It's like a beckoning
to unload the aching balls of my creative horn.
Then I remember,

Shit.
It's bin day.

I throw my coat on, shuffle out the back door,
dragging the wheelie bin behind me,
my breath a cold fog in front of my face,
thinking, *Well, at least I can look moody in the lane for a while.*

I look up at our window.
Mandy and the girls are waving at me.
All I feel is stupid, human love.
All I want is to dive back into bed with them,
sing songs and play.

I slap myself out of it, shout,

'C'mon, Chris! Stick with it!
Think!
What would you do
if you were in a Radiohead video, right now?'

Tearing off my clothes,
I run down the lane
in slow motion.

Shot of Mandy at the window, rolling her eyes.
I don't care.
I'm running
towards the river,
in the nude.
The stones are hurting my feet
but I tell myself the pain
is just part of my experience.

I can feel wind in my hair.
It feels like I've like got hair.

Shots of me throwing off metal shackles.
WAPOOOF!

I see our neighbour.
I raise my hand
to give him a victorious high five.
He thinks I'm waving.

'Morning.'

'Morning.'

I miss.
Awkward.

Keep running.
Nearly at the river now.

Keep running.

Keep running.

My right foot lands in a cowpat.
Straight through the crust
and into the fetid liquid beneath.
It's freezing.
I slide to a stop. Stand,
holding my shrivelled genitals,
shit between my toes,
stare at the water
and turn for home.

Mandy wraps a towel round me,
gives me a cup of tea.
Poppy says, 'Daddy's got poo feet.'
I nod,
hop upstairs.
Phil Collins is on the radio.
I can't help thinking,

Hmm. That's got a good beat.

SUPPERTIME

After Jazzy Jeff and the Fresh Prince

A hundred press-ups used to be a cinch.
Now I'm breaking sweat after ten, at a pinch.
Muscles stiff like wood. If I could I'd exchange them.
Laziness and gravity have conspired to rearrange them.

I used to have a six-pack, two hundred crunches with ease.
Now I've got a one-pack from all this cider and cheese.
Knees are like bobbles, like the knobbles in a Twiglet.
Belly was a rock, now it wobbles when I jiggle it.

Used to think I was hip, now I hop on the scales,
rockin' the defunct hairbrush as a mic.
I look pale in my pants in the mirror as I rhyme,
remixing Jazzy Jeff and Fresh Prince's 'Summertime'.

Here it is, a meal slightly transformed,
just a bit of a break from the norm,
just a little snack to break the monotony
of all these evening feeds that have gotten to be
a little bit mass-produced, it's cool to snack,
but what about a cheese that's so ripe it fights back?
Give me a crumbly blue fix
and if it tastes strong then don't try to mix it.
Think of the suppers of the past,
adjust your waste, you know fine foods last.
Pop in a cracker or three and uncork the wine
and put your napkin on and tuck in, 'cause this is suppertime.

GRAMMAR WARS WITH A TWO-YEAR-OLD

Lula: Are you got a dog, Daddy?
Me: Have you got a dog. It's 'have you got a dog, Daddy?'
Lula: Have you got a dog, Daddy?
Me: Good girl. No, I haven't.
Lula: I got a dog.
Me: Have you?
Lula: Yeeeees. He's very friendly. Let's go downstairs. You carry dog. I'll carry Ragdoll.
Me: OK.
Lula: Ragdoll's got a cold. *(To Ragdoll)* Are you got a cold?
Me: Have you got a cold?
Lula: No.
Me: No, I mean that's how you say it to Ragdoll.
Lula: I say it to Ragdoll.
Me: Yes, you say, 'Have you got a cold?'
Lula: Have you got a cold, Ragdoll? She got a cold. Aaaaah. I give her some medicine. Is she sad? Aaaaaah. It's OOOh-KAY. Are you got a cold, Daddy?
Me: No, I haven't, and it's 'have you'… never mind.
Lula: Are you is sad?
Me: No.
Lula: You are.
Me: OK.
Lula: Cry.
Me: Really?
Lula: YES, DADDY! CRY!
Me: *(sobbing noise)*
Lula: Are you is sad?
Me: Yes, I am. You don't need the 'is'.
Lula: Aaaahhh. It's OOOOh-KAY. I'll get some medicine.
Me: I don't really think I need medicine if I'm crying. Maybe just a cuddle.
Lula: Here's some medicine. There. Are you all better?
Me: Yes.
Lula: You're not, you're sad. Are you is sad?

Me:	OK.
Lula:	Cry.
Me:	*(sobbing noise)*
Lula:	Aaaahhh. It's OOOOh-KAY. I'll get some medicine. Here. All better. I went on the trampoline.
Me:	Did you?
Lula:	Yes. I spat on it.
Me:	Oh. Did you?
Lula:	Yes. Then I put my toes in the spit. It was funny. Are you got a spit, Daddy?
Me:	Have you got some spit. *(To self)* Is that right?
Lula:	Yes, I got some spit. Are you got some spit?
Me:	'Have you got some spit', that's what you say, I think, though we don't really ask that much.
Lula:	Have you got some spit, Daddy?
Me:	Good girl. Yes, I have. We've all got spit.
Lula:	I like spitting.
Me:	Mmm.
Lula:	I am going to the shops.
Me:	OK, good.
Lula:	You push me on my dog. Here's the shop.
Me:	What are we getting?
Lula:	Uhh, some sausages. Here, put them in your pocket.
Me:	OK. Anything else?
Lula:	No, you push me on my dog. Are you got a dog, Daddy?
Me:	Have you got a dog.
Lula:	Yeeees. Silly Daddy. I sitting on the dog.
Me:	No, you say 'have you got a dog', not 'are you got a dog'.
Lula:	Have you got a dog, Daddy?
Me:	Good girl. No, I haven't, but you have.
Lula:	Yes. Let's go to the shops. You push me on my dog.
Me:	OK.
Lula:	Here's the shop.

Me: What are we getting this time?
Lula: Uhhh, a tiny tiny fox.
Me: Interesting.
Lula: Here, you put it in your pocket. He's very small, be careful.
Me: OK. Anything else?
Lula: Uhh, yes. Coconuts and stories.
Me: Excellent choice.
Lula: Here, you put them in your pockets.
Me: OK.
Lula: Are you got coconuts and stories in your pockets?
Me: Have you.
Lula: Have you?
Me: Have I what?
Lula: Have you got coconuts and stories in your pockets?
Me: Good girl. Yes, I believe I have. And sausages and a tiny tiny fox.

Lula looks pleased and spits on the carpet.

PRAYER IN THE VALLEY

Crockle clock. Crockle clock.
Lone voice of yellow-legged hen.
Slow strut, peck and preen, amongst
orange trees, banana palm
and jasmine flowers.

Olympus soars in craggy splendour.
The steam of August's heat
drifts inland, like ghosts.
Nothing moves, bar bugs
and flies, flitting. Afternoon
slowness slugs on.

The muezzin's call to prayer
lights the air like a match,
his dry voice rising, echoing
around the mountain, like time itself.
When he sings, heart piped
through metal cone at top of tall tower,
beanstalk counterpoint
to broad onion dome, metal
shining so brightly the sun
itself is dazzled by its own reflection,
it's as if the silence thickens.
The whole valley listens.
The mountain contemplates
the gods of men and nods
benevolently, patience
etched into its strata.

The song ends.
A breeze
whispers through leaves.
A cockerel offers its riposte
and somewhere, far off,
a sleeping dog opens its eyes,
stands, barks
and pads off to drink.

PATRICIA

I remember you
when we were different shapes,
when discovery
smelled like Plasticine
and a pair of new Clarks shoes.

But before that,
I remember you
when I heard every one of your heartbeats,
when your breath was mine
and I was rocked,
sleeping, in utero.

And before that,
when I sat formless
behind your smile.

LIKE DRAGONS (BIRTHDAY LETTER TO SELF)

Forty-two years banging this drum.
Rhythms drift,
memories shapeshift,
words settle
just long enough to echo.

So what is it, now I'm here?

A hand that holds mine,
strokes me, squeezes shoulders, rings
on fingers – intertwined.
Radio heads.

Blue eyes – four pairs.
We dream in a pack,
waking to small soft exhalations.
Smiles break every day
wide open.

It's work,
solitude,
it's surprisingly nuclear.
It's communion,
play,
friends,
arms around shoulders.
Weekend pirates and rock stars,
love in our guitars,
one eye on the future
and its desperate promises. Beliefs
slain like dragons.

God's at the fancy dress shop.
God's at the theatre.
God is standing barefoot in wet grass
smoking a reefer, knowing
a moon is above her.
Aldrin's enduring footprints,
a compass scratch on a fourteen-year-old's arm.

It's all talk;
small talk, tall talk, fools' talk.
It's a moonwalk,
claiming the right
to dance like my dad,
now I am a dad.
No shame.
It's removing *should*
from my vocabulary
and *good*
and *bad*.
It's laughing
when I see my legs in the mirror.

It's being grateful.
We can pay the rent.
We can eat.

But what is it?

Not the angry passions of yesterday,
rough-hewn and reckless.
Not hot passions of heart and groin,
blind and breathless.

It is a warm sun in my chest,
a heavy hollow in my heart where the dead live,
a yes yes yes to every breath,
prayers for the dead,
thanks for the living.

It's giving
whatever I've got.

FIRES

Talking loud
in multiple voices,
we trade tumbles,
tickle, spin.
They climb me, fearless,
joy spitting from their mouths
in reckless bubbles,
speech abandoned
to high-pitched squeaks.

They slap my back,
squeeze my head,
leap at me
over and over,
like every charge is bellowing,
We've got NOW, Daddy,
we've got THIS!
Come ON! Let us
bite you. Let's blow
spit bubbles. You be
Alicia Keys. We'll ride
a horse. Her name's
Pam Pam. Let's go
to the beach,
to the atmosphere,
to the wolf's cave. Careful!
He's completely hungry.

When they are young women,
we will go out drinking.
And they'll leave me in the dust,
smiling through tears
as I wave
and watch them
set fire to the night.

THANKS AND ACKNOWLEDGEMENTS

Thank you to Clive Birnie for running a poetry publishing company like an independent record label. The world needs this. Or at least I do, and because I conflate myself with the world, I think therefore everyone does. Maybe that's something I need to look into. Anyway. Thanks for your patience and for doing this. Thanks also to Liv Torc and Harriet Evans for making the book look good and spotting all my mistakes. Thanks to all the poetry comrades who read drafts and gave me feedback in the making of this book and the writing of these poems; in particular, Anna Freeman, Adam Kammerling, Sally Jenkinson, Liv (again) and Jasmine Cooray. Thanks to David Cuesta at CR&D for the cover and for always making my work and that of Tongue Fu look so fine. Huge loving thanks to Mandy Redmond for supporting me through making this and to our girls Lula and Poppy. Without you three I wouldn't have half this material. Thanks for putting up with me at home and in my absence and for making me laugh every single day. Huge love and endless thanks to my parents, Peter – for the writing, drumming and performing genes – and Pat – for the wild spirit, bloody-mindedness and firm belief that anything is possible. And to the whole Redmond clan. We're very lucky.

These poems have been read all over the world, in/at pubs, basement bars, funerals, weddings, huge concert halls, dingy recording studios, festival stages, theatres, kitchens, tents, village halls, train stations and cafés. They have been read and heard in London, Bristol, Brighton, Dublin, Cardiff, Edinburgh, Galway, Johannesburg, Cape Town, Barcelona, Rio de Janeiro, Yeovil and Aldershot. Huge thanks to every promoter, producer, poet, hustler, audience member who has ever given me a gig, a pint, a place to stay, or offered kind words of encouragement. These exchanges mean the most. Props to Rich Mix, Roundhouse, Apples and Snakes, Poetry Can, Renaissance One, Arts Council England, British Council, Bristol Old Vic, The Albany, BAC, Take Art, London Wonderground, West End Centre, Hip Yak Poetry Shack, Bang Said The Gun, Hammer & Tongue, Outspoken, Chill Pill, One Taste, Raison d'Etre, Penned in the Margins, Lingo Festival – Ireland, Cúirt Literature Festival – Ireland, Word

N Sound – South Africa, FLUPP Literature Festival – Brazil, Kosmopolis – Barcelona, Glastonbury Festival, Big Chill, Latitude Festival, Camp Bestival, Bestival, Wilderness, Festival No. 6, WOMAD, Scarborough Fair, Kendall Calling, Standon Calling, Ledbury Poetry Festival, Bristol Poetry Festival, London Word Festival, Swindon Poetry Festival, Bath Poetry Festival, Gilded Balloon and Brett Vincent at Get Comedy. Thanks to Dan Gray at Get Involved for all your help. It's much appreciated. And thanks to Shane Solanki.

Massive thanks to the Tongue Fu crew for providing a constant challenge to enquire, take risks and improve. Riaan Vosloo, Patrick Davey, Arthur Lea, Belle Ehresmann, David Cuesta (again) and all the musicians who've come through – you are an inspiration. Thanks always to our dear gone friend Graham Fox for the years of smoke and thunder on the drums; we miss you. And thanks to every single poet I have shared a stage with, watched, read, taught, listened to and learned from. It's a peculiar affliction we have. Thanks for making it a constant source of wonder, confusion and inspiration.

Lightning Source UK Ltd.
Milton Keynes UK
UKHW011815200619
344748UK00002B/127/P

9 781909 136694